The good thing about learning
a new language is...
you must think

before you speak...

Jerry Marsh
Thanks a thousand times

Corner Stores

In The Middle Of The Block

That Urban Look

by

BLUE

Library Of Congress Catalog Number TXU887-348

International Standard Book Number ISBN 0-9712581-2-0

Published by **The Great Persuader Publishing**
P.O. Box 1100
New York NY 10030

Cover design and layout by Derrick Wilson

Printed In the United States of America

Thanks a lot to Lady Go, Mahogany Browne and Nicole Alexander

Much love to my baby Shaquila Ali

Acknowledgments

To Mr.Wilson and many men like him that don't always seem to say the right thing at the right time but deep in the corners of my mind I know he means well
Besides, he made David, Monica, Mike, and me so I know that there's a first time for everything and a second and a third and a fourth. And to Mrs. Wilson who was there listening
Auntie Debra I didn't forget you this time...

Don Turner, a world class and great boxing trainer but an even better mentor, you taught me a lot about life
Big Dee, Mel and Dale "Doppy Loppy" Martin from the Uptown Cut Master Daze

Thank you Fisiwe Cook who was always there with open arms,
Odell and the Sugar Shack family, Wizzo, Ngoma, Ras Tshaka Tongue, and Tantra, I didn't forget you pretty lady...
Thanks a thousand times. "I started writing poetry and I went to the Sugar Shack and I bumped into you, I was born for you."
E. Patrick, Brother Michael, Stew and the Brooklyn Moon, Harlem One Two Five, Ian Friday and the Tea Party family, Hayden The Blue Lion, Kool Breeze, Iyawo
Peace to a real brother Chris Slaughter, Brother Earl Majette, Shariff, Khasim Allah, Iyaba Mandingo and Adonis. Also there are so many great poets and writers that I have come in contact with and I want to thank you all. And I really mean it!

I would like to thank all the wonderful people that supported me when I was out there pushing the chap books, and I mean the strangers that knew nothing about me or never heard me recite
Yet, you bought the book anyway
"The BLUE Light Deluxe" Volume one
"The BLUE Light Deluxe" and "Just BLUE"
You all have been so good to me and I really mean it.
Even the ones that told me "NO." That just made me work harder...

Table Of Contents

Table Of Contents

Table Of Contents

Good Morning

A poem for Patty from the Church Street Deli
I hope you made it out

Don't get me wrong... the coffee is good
Even the bagels are great
They just can't compare to your smile
It's like a horizontal moon
It has put a bounce in my step
and added pleasure to my days
That's why I decided to take the long way to work today
Just to greet you with a smile
And tell you, "Good Morning"

Untitled

Close the bridges and the thruways into the Bronx and it would look just like a concentration camp

It already looks like a makeshift reservation and the only thing missing are the casino's and valet parking...

But I know once they built that middle class coffee shop in the heart of Black Mecca...the rent would go up

That was the whole purpose of Crack being pumped into the neighborhood

It was to pimp the misery of the working poor, and eventually Harlem would be a playground for the Bougies

Then it would be just like Jamaica

It would be just like Puerto Rico

It would be just like any other Caribbean Island where there's a hotel or resort that separates the Have from the Have not's and if anybody ever spoke about social injustice or racial equality, they would simply be classified as a nut case... Just like me

But who remembers Marcus Garvey?

Who remembers when those crooked cops shoved a wooden stick up that mans rectum and the media insisted that he was sexually assaulted?

But the Rectum is not a sex organ...

It don't reproduce

Its word play - that plays on the patriotic passion of the average American with subliminal messages and subconsciously we're taught to believe that everybody named Muhammad is an enemy

It won't be long before we start teaching our children that the solar eclipse and earth quakes are linked to terrorism

All while we're quoting verse from the bible, we have the audacity to sing the national anthem…and that's a big contradiction

That's just like having smoke detectors inside of a Tee pee and we're passing around Peace Pipes- wondering why is the alarm is going off….

But ya'll know the ole sayin'…
           Where there is smoke….

Going To Philly

Unseen words carry no weight, but they can be heavy
They leave dents in my mind if I don't speak my mind,
that's why it's a must that I... speak my mind

If not I can't sleep at night
It's like having bricks in my bed
There's a war going on inside of my head and a truce is necessary so I speak up!
I be spitting in Ebonics when I be chilling with my people
We be conversing in a language that some might consider unfit for corporate America
That's when everybody wants to be somebody
Everybody wants to feel important but they're not willing to endure the rigors of the mission
We can't sit home watching television and think welfare is going to rectify our condition
Fronting like celebrities - making babies on top of babies and we can't feed the ones we already have
We can make room for our rat's and roaches
and our pit bulls make a nice bed for our pet fleas
At the end of the week we buy beer and dog food with Food stamps while the children get a balanced breakfast of potato chips and Kool-Aid

In The Middle Of The Block

Everybody is trying to get rich quick, playing Quick Pick
but the next man is always the winner
That game makes money off poor people's misery
Misery loves company and that's why people that live alone
talk a lot!

I didn't get here in an inner tube just to become shark bait
over the Atlantic...*I was born here!*
In the core of the apple, at the pit of the borough
I hung out with the rejects and the down trodden
But this city was rotten before I was begotten
So I ask you, am I the eye sore just because I saw rats bigger than cats and a cool cat was the terminology to describe a friend
Back in '76
Now he's my dog
My girl is my bitch and my friends are my niggers...

I live underneath the under, at the bottom of the low
I was eavesdropping on Army ants tryin' to find a source of
unity
I bought a bus ticket but I couldn't take it to the hereafter
so I just settled in Philly, but when I got there the same bullshit was
going on, so I came back and the minute I stepped off the bus all I
could hear was, "excuse me, Brother
Pardon me, Black
Do you have a quarter?
Do you have a nickel?
Do you have a dime?
Do you have a cigarette?
Do you have a light?
Do you have the time?
Pray to Jesus
Pray to Jehovah
Pray to Jah

Pray to Allah
Pray to Guiliani because he thinks he's God !11"
99.9 percent of the people in this world are convincing
back stabbers!

"Don't eat sugar
Don't eat salt
Don't eat pork
Don't eat meat
Save the dolphins
Save the whales
Save the children
Save the rain forest."

Time out, if life is a game, who's playing?
If we're a race, whose winning?

Being that we're at the door step of technology, Scientists
are trying to mock the womb of a woman and create children
without the act of sex
Viagra will be for some rich fuck that just wants to get his
dick up, jack off in a jar... and then freeze his bastards to insure he
has an heir to his crown

Everyone listen up... Every mind is a world and only you can
make you happy, just don't bother me with it!!!

That's why I stopped giving my money to bums!

I got tired of them throwing my pennies in the street
Then they act like they don't want to eat the food that I try
to give'em
Don't you know this one bum told me he's a vegetarian!
He went on to say that life had thrown him a curve ball

I think he was trying to use me to get a hit

Bad habits stay on the shoulders of the rejects that wait for a check...then get upset when the mailman is late

Conflicts occur in the front lobby but he was the same guy that had the hobby just like he's was a millionaire, with sneakers piled up to the ceiling

buying a new pair when the first pair got dirty...

But now he's begging!

Contrary to popular belief, you can't get rich selling drugs because a decent lawyer is expensive

But in every state there's a ghetto and in every ghetto there's a corner and on that corner there's somebody thinking that they can defy the odds...

I guess its O.K. to sell death to the people as long as you *"Keep It Real"*

Because when you're *"Keeping It Real"* that then gives you a reason to be part of the problem

People will go and protest police brutality but won't say anything about the pusher

That's because they know the pusher personally and he's just *"Keeping It Real"*

We call each other brothers...then we kill over colors and mug one another for chump change

And it's never enough change to change our standard of living but then we sit back and complain "that nobody gives a damn about the people in the hood!!!"

But what about the preachers and their fashion conscious congregation?

It's funny how black people had it all before segregation now it's like we don't have jack to show for it but a sign that reads: BUY BLACK

    We call each other niggers and figure the bigger the gun the bigger the boy because he's the one that sits home watching TV

    Someone has him believing he's a straight up "GEE", so he keeps his right hand in his pocket and it's the same hand that he smacked his girl with

    It's the same hand that he describes his words with
And it's connected to his trigger finger and it's all a bullshit concept of

Keeping It Real!

Brown Paper Bag

The guy don't make the girl and the girl don't make the guy but once they form a common bond you then have something special

Understand that I am not saying this just to be in someone's favor but it's like my girl, she's at the center of my circumference
She's the focus of my determination to have a Blue nation and a generation full of kids... that I'll teach to behave like children

I'm going to paint a flag with her face on it as a symbol of our alliance and I'll mark our territory with the sweet fragrance of her shampoo

My girl has a brown paper bag complexion...
Light skinned by black folks standard

But there's a deep dark richness that I really dig about her

She has a sense of humor that could crack a smile on a cloud
Brighten up my day making way for light
She brightens up the dark tunnels inside of me
Jokingly with me one day she said, *"roaches are related to vampires..."* The reason being is she said, "*because roaches are hard to kill, like vampires... and roaches are afraid of light, like vampires...*"
But hey, she's my flower and she can make bees bug out!

She can make bluebirds give bear hugs to blackbirds and they would engrave her name on the bark of an evergreen tree just to spread the word that a new flower is in town

And somehow precious metal just has no value compared to my rose petal

She makes me want to go knee level
Scuba dive in between her thighs
embrace her hips and drink her loving... *like dip!*

I wish that I could put some in a bottle and save some for tomorrow

Or just freeze it, put her face on a label and it'll be like ice cream

We have pet names for our private parts

We sometimes pondered foreplay in public places and provocative subjects always seem to pop up in a low-lit restaurant

We like having conversation over coffee
Talking about poetry

And she has lyrics like literature that just drip from her bottom lip and I'd jump to catch every drop with my index finger

And being a student of body language, she knows me better than I know myself

So whenever I said "NO"

She said that really means "yes"

And whenever I said "YES" she said that really means to "go faster"

Sometimes she would begin to demonstrate the mechanics of auto-eroticisms with my middle finger

So you see, you can't judge your relationship on some luke warm love affair

Or something that you've seen on the soaps because that

eventually goes dry

That's like tumbleweed tumbling on ice which was brought to New York by some tourist from Texas that came to take notes and the tumbleweed as a token of appreciation for what they learned

So in spite of the jealousy and envy we still continue to shine

Even if we were walking down a one-way, dead end street

Some might say that's the wrong direction but it doesn't make a difference as long as I have my reflection with me

That's the girl with the Brown Paper Bag complexion...

Well, light skinned by black folks standard...

Haiku

Spring Flower

She's my spring flower

and I'm losing altitude

Help! May Day... Mayday

I wrote this while sitting in a night club on 125th Street and Manhattan Avenue... It was right after a Poetry slam

Ladies Night

R ight there!

Right there is where she sat
It was in the corner of this little smoke filled nightclub
This is where the people threw their body sweat up against the wall as they danced and waved their hands up in the air

It was like they were cutting slices of pie into this thick white cigarette smoke

This was the same smoke smell that I knew I was going to carry home tonight in my brown leather coat
Mixed with the BLUE Water cologne that I had on under my arm pit
I had a hint of brandy on my breath... *but luckily I had a peppermint*
And that girl, she sat in the center of her two girlfriend and they were slapping high-fives and giving each other a toast as they celebrated their freedom

It was a Friday

It was the ladies night

On the tables were salt and pepper shakers

Empty ashtrays and a candlelight that did the electric slide across the tip of her nose

And the light highlighted her foundation

Her eyeliner

Her lipstick and it put a BLUE streak through the center of her jet-black hair

ME?

Well I sat alone at a table that was meant for two and I was admiring the girl in the middle

I think it was the way she bit her bottom lip and took sips of her daiquiri

She bounced to the mellow beats as she swayed from left to right

She persuaded me to write and if she had a preconceived notion about me... I hope it was right

So I wrote her a note and the note read: *"You know that there are just some days when I just don't feel like getting out of bed and then I realized that only bums sleep late and that's a luxury I just can't afford*

Every dime I make... belongs to you!"

M A C K   M E!!!

She smiled and we talked for a while and the conversation grew and everything... and I mean everything about this girl I almost knew

She was 29 and fine, Sex appeal and all, the whole nine

Her body was banging!!!

And I didn't give a damn about her mind

She just had this kind of shape that could stop time and time couldn't put it's hands on her

She had an hourglass figure and the way I figured... she'd

probably make me come quicker than a loaded gun...
    with a hairy trigger

    So I said to myself, "bet, if she gives me some... I'ma just close my eyes and concentrate real hard, on some body ugly...
    and I mean Reeeeal ugly"

    Now, the only thing that could stop her and I from doing this and that was... What if? But then again hey, why not?

    And for all these thoughts we entertained if they became reality who should I thank?
    God...
    Or the devil?

    Mannnn, we went back to my place and it felt like she was adding youth to my bones

    We started to melt like candles at a cheap hotel in Rome
    Our thoughts ran parallel, we skipped right over the paradox of dinner being the contract for sex

    Pretty Lady U R my religion!!!

    And if you should ever leave, pleeeease take my soul but you got to leave that smile

    Kiss me and give me your cold and I'll carry it like it's a style

    Stop up my sink when you wash your hair and that's just to mark your territory and I can say that you were here!!!

    You can leave your T-shirt

Corner Stores

You can leave your underwear
You can leave your hat
Leave something so I'll know that you'll be back
As a matter of fact you can tattoo your name across my chest because my heart you just crushed and you can write your initials if you're in a rush...

It's just one thing I need to know before you go
Pretty Lady...

What 'Cho Name Is???

This poem was written after I listened to the Ghetto locker room lawyers. And this poem was the outcome

What The Deal Is?

Out Of Style is a name of town that just happens to be on the opposite side of this town and ironically you have to drive In-Style just to get out

Me? Well, I set the trends there
It always happens by accident when I get dressed in a hurry
Can't you tell...?

The reason I asked you that is because I haven't seen myself in a while

Sometimes I forget what I look like
Photographs show me flashes of what was but my memories become to heavy too hold
However taxi cabs... they will give your ass a wake up call
They will give you a reality check
Every time I hop in a cab and request to be taken to the opposite side of town
The reply is always "No!"
And when I ask the cab driver, "why?"

He says, "Because it's too far Out Of Style right now."

Out Of Style is where the men boast to believe in God, yet they walk around pussy whipped and comfortable being poor
Grabbing their dicks while they Diddy Bop and holding conversations that are condensed into hand gestures
"Ya know what I'm saying?"

It's like *Keeping It Real* is a past time
It's much like Baseball and Fishing
While the faithful in Harlem, go fishing for potential disciples
They start to pull pamphlets from under their armpits just to show me their depiction of heaven
They said that, "The lion would sit with the Lamb in the hereafter"

And I'm like, what? *R U telling me - that the king of beast becomes a vegetarian?*
And they'll go grazing on the open plains of new Asia?
And they won't even joust with the wildebeest? And warthogs for fruits and berries?

Then I asked, "So what's the big deal about the discovery of electricity or the invention of the light bulb?"
Harlem is my depiction of hell and vacant lots have become playgrounds
That's where flies go to play
That's where lighting bugs lie around lackadaisical in an air of their own arrogance once they've realized they are in control of the spotlight!
As for me, I told them that I can hear the moon rise at night
I've seen the sun shine in an ultra violet BLUE light and I can read the diverse languages of water

I can put the palm of my hand into the Atlantic Ocean

and read the waves, like Braille
    I've sent messages to the Sub Sahara on the backs of
eagles and it was like, E-mail...

I am God!!! If you don't believe me just ask my daughter

    Man is the Supreme Being while the world waits for a
U.F.O's to come save our souls and the scientists know ain't nothing out there

    How come scientists can send a search warrant to Pluto and
they can't find a cure for the common cold?

    They can't find a cure for AIDS
    They can't find a cure for cancer
    So red necks rush just to get melanin shots, try'n to block
the UV rays
    And Black folks are still getting hair perms... (and that's
cool)
    But then they have the nerves to tell me that their grandpar-
ents were Indians!

    But they just have hopes that one day they'll be able to fit
into America's stream
    And they dream of the days that they'll be able to purchase
bean pies and apple pies at concession stands during Yankee games

    So ya see...no matter what "The Tiger" said about his color
he'd still have a hard time catching a cab in style
    And if he catches it Out Of Style, he'll be asked to pay up
front just like everybody else in the hood!
                    So what da deal is?

Hope?

Hope is this four letter word that was spoon-fed to the hungry- it was done in an effort to sustain their hunger, temporarily

It's similar to welfare

It's like getting just enough but it's never enough to get you over the hump of the every day living

Yet in the meantime we continue to trot back and forth to that high priced, belligerent bodega on the corner

That's where the clerk behind the counter is considered cool Just because his name is Muhammad and he'll let you go for a penny when you're short

Muhammad doesn't mind because he's going to get the penny right back as soon as he charges 99 cents for a particular product and the big shots are always too busy to wait for their change

Muhammad is The Man
and he always washes his hands before he prays

You just have to remind him to wash his hands as soon as he comes out the bathroom and he tries to make you a sandwich

This bodega is the first stop in the morning for the students that attend the middle school right across the street

They go there for the salt and sugar sandwich because they're kosher and they get a glow-in-the dark soda for an extra fifty cents

And then there's Mrs. Wilson, the 7th grade teacher and she can never figure out why the students are always so sleepy so early in the morning, especially her pet student, Wanda

Wanda is 13 going on 30 and that fits right into the family budget because Wanda and her mother have the same taste in clothing and I guess that's why she's caught the eye of her mother's boyfriend
That creep sits around all day with a dingy straw hat on and a cheap leisure suit in the middle of October
He has a gold tooth in the middle of his mouth and he smiles all day just to show that gold tooth off!!!

This guy is always mumbling under his breath about how he thinks Wanda is built like a brick and he said it's got to be something in the milk "because milk does the body good"

I can hear the drama take place each morning from the family that lives above me...
They live in the basement
I live underneath them!!!
I live next door to the devil and he has a dog that he loves more than he loves himself
He never cleans up after the dog, leaving the dog shit right in the doorway, hoping to give me good luck for the following weeks
Sometimes I work the graveyard shift and the same faces I see at night, I see in the morning... Chilling!
That's what the guys on the corner call it and out of fear that if they move, they might fall off the face of the earth

So they stand there all day and night just passing time and telling tales about how they were running things when they were locked down up north

And I'm thinking to myself, why don't they run the locker room lawyers off the street that are so convinced that the same Jesus that walked the earth 2000 years ago is going to walk bare footed down Malcolm X Blvd and resurrect the dead

And if he is, he must have changed his name to *Je'sus a*nd he likes to wear his hat turned to the back with his pants hanging off his ass

I think that's ass backwards but hey, that's *Je'sus*

Je'sus has got to come at night like they prophesied because if he comes in the morning all the crack heads will still be asleep and they'll be mistaken for dead

(And then they're going to miss their blessing)

But up until then, the drug kingpins will be the spokesmen for the neighborhood and they're going to help us lead a protest against police misconduct

The only problem is the guys from Brooklyn don't want to go to Harlem and the guys from Harlem don't want to go to Brooklyn

And it seems the only common ground they share is that they think the Bronx Zoo is located in Queens

In the midst of all this confusion, tourists come through the hood on a tour bus and they start looking at us like they couldn't believe we can speak and we only communicate through singing and dancing...

Then from out of nowhere comes a bum and he tries to squeegee the bus window

Then bus driver gets upset and a fight breaks out!

all this confusion had the tourists worried, but we're working it out and we'll go for a bite to eat
Me, the squeegee man, the tourists

We'll have macaroni with cheese, collard greens, and corn bread and we'll stuff it all inside of a work boot

Now that's what I call sole food...

I wrote this poem with no shirt on while standing in front of a mirror practicing facial expressions
I was home alone and there was no fear of my being seen
But it's these kinds of thoughts that help me maintain my sanity
Maybe one day we can all meet in space and let our minds collide, providing that we give each other some space from time to time
Because time is the author of life and life is for the living and when we meet again we'll live it up like we did the last time
But up until then... "B"
I'm going back around the block and wait for Je'sus
We got this protest going
and we're trying to get the street named after him

Peace!

My life
The page listed,   not

Last night was the night that I decided to cut the wings off of this madness and since I stopped getting high my feet are flat on the ground and now I realized that I'm walking the earth with the general public and it's a bunch of pissed off people...like Me!!!

Here I am sharing this congested city sometimes wondering why wasn't I aborted?

Is it because religion speaks out against that?

But does this world need one more passive person catering to the needs and the wants of the aristocrat?

For as long as I continue to get my ass kicked while sitting in the back of the bus singing *"We Shall Overcome"* God is going to look out for me?

And you're say, "Yes" because God does not like ugly

So now I'm asking what about pigs?

They're ugly and they get eaten every day, for breakfast, lunch and dinner

And Jeffrey Dahmer has proven that you can eat steamed black ass and still survive

So now I'm asking how many children come into this world

Born Black - Strike One
Born Poor - Strike Two

Born in a society where a black child's only aspiration is to become a ball player... Instead of a thinker?

And he's taught to believe that as long as he prays hard enough his dreams will come true

But this God that we pray to has a funny way of showing us that he loves us because most churches are filled with a bunch of backstabbing people...seeking redemption...Like Sister Shirley

Sister Shirley is the one that once had the high price tag on her private parts and she would talk trash to every man that she's ever dated
And that's because she knows that the second she calls the police, they're going to come to the house
kick her door down
Kick her boyfriend in the ass, then put a box cutter in his pocket
Just to have a reasonable cause for leaving her Boy friend bloody

She's the one that you see in the supermarket with a shopping cart full of food and the food only requires hot water and the I. Q. of a wet cat to prepare
So all of her grown ass children that still live with her instead of eating at the same time, decide to eat in shifts...one after the other
Fuckin' up the kitchen and leaving the sink full of dishes
And it's always the next person's responsibility to clean it up!!!

And now that Sister Shirley is a little bit older and her ass is not as round as it used to be...
She can't use it as a tool to reel the men in like she once did
Now she goes in search of a religion and she joins a church
And she'll be sitting in the front rostrum next to Brother James, the X Alcoholic

And she'll be telling Brother James about her adult son, the one that just went and bought a brand new car instead of getting out of his mother's house and paying rent for himself

But Sister Shirley loves her baby
And she said, "God is going to see a way for her one day"

But that's the very reason I can't see myself sitting next to a bunch of passive people
Seeking redemption for all the backstabbing shit that they've learned in the streets
Then after a long day of praying, they'll turn around and try to screw me in the brain
In the name of the Lord!!!

Then I'll be considered the bad guy, just for speaking my mind!
But that's what I have a mind for and my only crime is saying what I feel
And I'll continue to be this way until I'm old and decrepit and the weight of a one-ounce ink pen bares a burden on my wrist
Then I'll be a one-toothed bastard sitting in the corner of my house spitting blood in the center of my book on life just because I'm just pissed off that I can't stop my hands from shaking!!!
And then maybe...just maybe I'll meet some fine young soul and hopefully she'll keep me young when she looks into these cloudy brown eyes and tune in to my thoughts and record my thinking
But up until that great day, I'll be the white sheep of the family
I'll be that one guy that couldn't get a single dime from no one in my family to help get my ideas off of the ground,
But if I was to die right now... that's when they'll spend about six thousand dollars just to bury me

That's when Rev. Pig Foot and Pastor Hambone are going to come over and give their best tear-jerking sermon, milking my family for every dime that they have left

That's when all of my so-called friends are going to be there just so they can start fighting over my clothes and colored TV and everything else that can't fit into my casket

That's when I'm going to scream out loud from the grave and tell them all that they are full of shit!

And a bunch of fools for not just putting me in the ground and let the worms suck the rickets off of my balls

The birds are going to eat the worms and you can eat the birds and life as I know it will go on

Or maybe

Just maybe I'll fertilize the soil and speak through the trees and the breeze blowing off of the Hudson River will send chills up some young poets spine

Then He

Or She

Or it will find a creative way to write

Then that will be living proof that a dead BLUE is still alive and this is my life…

Haiku
Friends and Family!

Friends and Family
only call when they need me...

That's how they show love

Eaves Dropping on Yuri

A t the first sight of her pretty face she gave me butter-
flies... that chose to stay confined to the dark spaces
of my stomach and tickled my rib cage

I am now like a cocoon with legs, understanding the language of a newborn baby

He's just begging to return to the safety of his mother's
womb
Panicking at the first sight of light... and I can relate
I felt born again the first time that I laid eyes on you
and if by chance we should ever speak and my speech seems
slurred
It's only because you got me slightly punchy

You shook my equilibrium with your Ethiopian eyes and
if I was asked to describe the first time that I saw you, I could do
it in detail

How could I forget that June mist?

That slight humid breeze that made ripples over water
filled potholes on cobblestone Brooklyn streets

Footprints left behind by the natives that frequent the corners still carried a fresh scent to them as they seem to lead back to the Lion's den and Bear caves on State Street
The three-story brownstones,with large windows had no curtains, no venetian blinds

Combination is the name of a racehorse that has seen his best days and now he watches my fingertips from an antique oil painting
The sorrowed expression on his face tells me that he's unable to escape the borders of the colonial wood frame

 This is Yuri's place
Unintentionally an owl told me so
He keeps a journal on her and absent-minded he left it in the cavity of a Dogwood tree
In detail he describes her Persian rug with the red and gold streaks
The redwood coffee table with precisely cut unicorns at the base of the lampshade,
and the Grandfather clock that stopped at 6:06 and hasn't moved in months

5:01 PM: Religiously my angel is on time and she moves like a myth
She drops her purse on the floor and kicks her shoes off hooking her leather coat on the back of the door knob
(Too tired to be spooked by superstitions)
She motions with her remote control and hits her favorite CD and Roach begins to beat on the wall while Cliff swings on his name and Yuri continues to move like a myth...

9:00 PM: She'll begin to lotion her legs to the glow of the northern star while the moon rests on my head like an ice pack

I am a journeyman in deep water

Receiving instruction from my conscience

While fighting my ego

I'm a stranger in a familiar place

Eaves dropping on Yuri

That Girl

ummer time...these days were made for women... It's when they dress the best, It's when they wear less... It's when that summer breeze be blowing through that linen dress and it be giving me chills...
Making me sneeze... and she be blessing me!

Knowingly or unknowingly
Especially when she's pressing up against my chest and I loved her best when she was expecting

But it would be selfish for me to say that I wish that she could stay that way because the burden is on her back and that's not my back and I have to deal with her mood swing
When she starts transforming from a butterfly into a bat and then back into a butterfly

This was the poem that led me to write Miss Gravity and The Oblique Hints
I was riding on the uptown A train and for a minute I thought I was taking it to heaven
She was all wrapped up in the wings of a love story and when I saw the beauty of her unnatural face I wanted to beg the conductor to make a U turn

(Do you care?) If so, feel free to continue....
Her heart was cold,

It was like a final resting place for lost souls and Eskimos

who tried to hang with her and they froze to death!
  I was once the man of this house, but now I'm the mouse
getting beat by the cat that lied between her lap and once she stole
a part of me...all she left was a composite sketch of her face,
and it stayed stuck in my memory!

  What is it about her that makes me talk to myself,
when she's not in my presence?
  And even in my subconscious state I find myself concentrating on the middle of her
  She gave me balance

  I must of fallen asleep lying underneath her
  And then I woke up smelling like her...and our pets could-
n't even tell us apart

  I've had dreams that I put her earrings into candy
machines and I watched dimes fall out

  I was willing to empty all my fountain pens and refill
them with the blood that flows through my veins just to write her
letters

  But all those letters went unread and they serve no pur-
pose now but to be abrasive toilet paper,
  Stopping up my commode and that's a replica of my soul
            I NEEDED TO FLUSH HER OUT!
            I WANTED TO CURSE HER OUT!
  SOME TELL ME THAT I TALK TOO MUCK'N FUCH
                But what the...?

  She B Kris-crossing my days and jig-sawing my nights,
  She's got me puzzled
  She's got me jaywalking across the driveway

Corner Stores

She's got me catwalking   across the runway of an airport
She's got me traveling...on basketball courts,
And this is all due to lack of concentration
I'm busy concentrating on what light might sound like or
what sound might look like
I'm busy wondering how do the deaf communicate with
the blind?

The Password Is Yes

I don't want the bread... I want the butter
I don't want the coffee... I want the sugar

Sex...never constituted as a means of an even exchange for
money
It does not pay the bills!
Yet hypocritical I'm standing here thinking,
what's the purpose of my right hand when I can call you?

Let me find out that you're in the centerfolds of my maga-
zines and I'm up!
I marvel over the magic and beauty of your body
Sugar you are thick...
D E L U X E ! ! !

Tonight, we can sleep with the lights on and your voice
will be that song that vibrates in my stomach

Thunder is a light word and it would do no justice if I
tried to describe the impression you left on me

I guess the only reason that I never dream about you
Is because I stay up all night just thinking about you...

Your thoughts are my thoughts and they must be wrapped
in wool because they make me sweat...

43

If you touch me with your bath water and I'll confess all of my thoughts

I'll even die for the ones that other men contemplate when they see your face
Call me selfish, but I just can't imagine the thought of you being embraced by another and he's touching that thing,
That thing you just said belongs to me...
Y O U R   V E E E E E !
You make my screams of passion go pass the heavens and they echo in orbit
It's like I receive messages from distant galaxies and I have visions of falling stars

You must be the architect that designed orgasm with the foundation built on lust

I'll keep the BLUE prints to it all locked in my heart
And the Password Is Yes!!!

Southern Belle the money is on the dresser I'll keep the receipt under my pillow
And the next time I call, you'll know it's me
Because all I'll say is, yes

The original title was going to be "Ode To A Lap Dance"

O Magic

can tell the way that they watch you, that they have a thing for you...

They're probably wondering what it is that I do to you
Or how can they have you
I bet they wonder how do I do you or how do you do me
They don't understand that I've seen you prior to the cold cream and cocoa butter that only enhances your pretty dark brown complexion
I saw you sleep on your face and the pillow left prints on yo cheeks and you were still sweet - to me
I hope like hell it's voodoo that you put on me, just to give some logic as to why I love you the way I do

I've always felt that there is something sexy and erotic about a Sunday morning and I don't know if she knew it or not but that day, she picked the right time to touch me
She kept parading back and forth with nothing on but a soft cotton, French cuff link light blue dress shirt that covered her completely
And she left just enough of herself uncovered to excite my senses
I think if she would have sat 10 feet away from me that day and not touched me and me not touch myself
I still would have been able to get an orgasm... Just from my thoughts

45

Thinking about the times previously when she kissed me and sucked on me with ice cubes in the corner of her mouth

Sometimes pretending that my private parts were part of a standard shift race car and we were going into overdrive
Love, it's a must that we do this in slow motion and loco-motion and the love potion is the perspiration that settles in the center of a woman's middle
Teaspoons of that no calorie
fat free
strictly organic
Well you know!!!
It's the key ingredient for removing pimples
Shyness,
body blemishes
and it helps to stimulate the growth of my facial hair
What's interesting to me is, she never noticed the organic magic
Until I showed her
It was that day we stood face to face
And back to face as we vibrated in harmony
Leaving prints of our shoulder blades up against those wall to wall mirrors

I couldn't even imagine the Garden of Eden being any sweeter
It's like we fashioned that Sunday morning into a gospel song and I was so caught up into the Holy Ghost
That I went home... with no underwear on

But I had hers in my right hand and I was sniffing them all the way to the subway station

Lady I can live on the out skirts of your space and survive just fine off of the vapors of your breath

Inhaling every unseen molecule of your genetic make up and exhale every toxin that would make an attempt to pollute my system, telling me what I feel is only temporary

I must have you here, next to me, even if you're just sleeping
I can listen to your sub-conscience conversation that concern me not and I'll retort
Our days are like we're making porno tapes and we're testing the discipline of a celibate Pimp or a Ho
We can film our show in the center ring of a circus because nature knows how you bring out the animal in me
A freak for you I am He
I enjoyed seeing the envy in the twisted eyebrows of my enemies after they realized that you and I were wrapped up together
We unwounded together
We got high together
We got down together
You got my world rotating so fast and that includes light and sound and when I think that I'm only peeping at you, well staring becomes inevitable...

Haiku

Love Is Sweet

"Love is sweet" said she

The echoes of her whispers

Vibrate in my heart

The Movement

Friendly fire is the bullet that killed the innocent bystander who waited for a job to come and knock on his door while he spent his recreational time, watching TV

Complacent with the roof over his head he breaks his neck breaking his bread all for the apartment that he'll never own
While fulfilling his lord's dream... The landlord
The guy that exits the pearly gates of heaven that surrounds the land of milk and honey where Black folks aren't allowed
For they are lactose intolerant and lead the nation in diabetes

I'm from that part of town where there are *corner stores*
In the middle of the block
Run by men that left their ladies overseas
They took flight to America, abandoning their lifestyle and now they live this different lifestyle...

They try to make a dollar out of fifteen cents

And rap to hot headed crack heads and get a blow job for 10 dollars and 75 cents

And they figure10 dollars is for her Wash-n-Set

50 cents for a bag of potato chips and Quarter water

It's like artificial dye is added to the essence of life
It's like cows drinking Similac
It's like the dog feces that covers the concrete of these mean New York City streets

This is where the dogs and cats live better than the residents of a third world country and the presidents that run these countries are always at the top of the food chain

But what really bugs me out is how football games used to run these half time commercials and they try to make me feel like I'm the blame for somebody in one of these distant lands starving! And the commercial read:

"Tonight, somebody in this land will go another night without eating"

Yet I'm thinking the same thing is taking place where I'm from

UNDERSTAND that Revolutionary Movements and Bile movements both run parallel

It's when men long for a sudden change but they're not willing to fight for the cause, 'cause they fear that they might get their new Timberlands scuffed up

So they wait for a job to come knocking on the door while spending their spare time watching TV

Yet this is The land of the free, The home of the brave

This is the country were foreigners continue to land
and they work like slaves for minimum wage

Frying chicken in our kitchens and they couldn't believe
that Americans had the audacity to own garbage cans

Understand that garbage cans serve no purpose in their
land
Because nothing goes to waste and everything taste like
chicken when you're starving...

Haiku
Back Pain

Senior citizens
wearing shoes with velcro straps...

Rheumatism hurts!

Free Dome

Free your mind

B ack during 1555, A black woman's menstrual cycle didn't mean shit 'cause cotton was in high demand and the fallen sun was like the dead line

But my baby and me, we's got this crib on Mr. Will's plantation and sometimes he calls me his son and before you all knew me as *BLUE* People would address me as Mr. Will's-son

But me and my baby, we's gon' get hitched

See we's gon' jump the broom, but we's gon' to wait for the first full moon and that's only cuz the priest on the plantation never recognized me as a human

3/5th of a man is what he said that I wuz and that's the same debate that Jane had with Tarzan when she tried to justify her lust for that pet chimpanzee named Cheetah!

And that gave true meaning to the phrase having *Jungle fever* when she got caught doing the wild thing with a monkey in the back of the bushes

(It's said that AIDS originated in Africa)

It's also said that it's easier for a camel to get through the eye of a needle than it is for a man to enter the gates of heaven

Yet the preacher said "*Heaven is a higher manifestation of living*" And you got to die to get there... But I just don't want to go that high!

You can call me impatient, but I want my flowers now

Besides, I don't see anybody giving up their goods to come in the hood and live next door to me
Yet I see everybody in the hood dressing like they're rich
With a pocket full of lotto tickets and to me that's slavery!!!

Now Big Brother is watching over my back like an overseer and everybody wants to tell me that the New Jersey Path train is my way to freedom?

Ladies and Gentlemen, Ya gotta' set your dome free

'Cause Freedom of speech is the way to release steam and tension is a tight rope, so I tread lightly
But I think that someone put soap up under my feet
I slipped up and let my enemies know that they had me tripping
I tried to be slick - treat'em like a lady and buy them a new pair of shoes... hoping that they'd walk out of my life

What the hell did I step into?

THE YEAR WAS 1983 and I was saying goodbye to the guy's on the block and 8 hours later I was in Stuttgart, Germany and it was like culture shock

Classmates were making mockery of my facial features
and this New York accent and rich white women like Michael Jaxson didn't help the "proud to be black" slogan
He was like this Trojan horse trying to sneak through America's stage doors, up until some big stagehands told him to "Beat it kid!"
Moonwalk your light brown ass back to Africa

Go and sing, "We Are The World" to those brothers from the Sudan

The ones that appeared to be starving...

But actually they were full

They were just living off of the fat reserve left in their sperm with just enough strength to make one more baby

Now they smuggle their stamina into New York

And that's to help them run in marathons with no shoes on

New runners felt the vibration of the M. T. A. at the bottom of their feet, so they dropped in the middle of the street and started to pray

They were in fear that the noise at the bottom of their feet was the return of Mahdi...

but it wasn't... it was just the uptown A- train!!!

Derrick is the man that said religion should be put in a funnel and there would be one and I would be the sum and you validate me as your God and if that doesn't work, then we'll just become slaves to our labor

Kept in bondage by food chains with a food chain mentality where minimum wage is the max and taxes are going to take most of that

So here's The Deal...

I just want the world to think on their own without the thought of hands up their backs and strings on their fingers

And we'll listen to music that sounds like static and a "No" is automatic whenever someone expects me to dance

I'm going to pull my pants up until my belt touches my chest

I'm going to walk fast but take short steps

I'm going to read the mind of the lady that can read my mind and all she'll want is a quickie, with no strings attached

We'll never make love and have sex every day
And we'll have a bunch of bad ass kids and I'll teach them to play in the dark
And that's because I'm never going to pay my light bill
I'm never going to say, "Good Morning"
Or ask, "How are you?" because I'm not really going to care
I'm going to hate what you like
Like what you hate
Smile when I fight
Fight my sleep
And sleep with one eye open

I'm going to have that crazy ass house on the block
And when the cops come knocking
I'm going to claim to be victim of culture shock
And if they take the case to court
I'll guarantee you that I beat it!!!

This was the first poem that I ever wrote □Symbol of love.□
The first poem That I ever recited on open mic Was entitled □Every mind is a world□
And until this very day I can□t seem to find that poem

Symbol Of Love

Until I met you my life just didn't seem quite complete, but now that you're with me I'm going to lay heaven at your feet
If there were no God, I'd worship you
Are you sure you didn't put the stars in the sky?
It just seems like something you would do
You're more precious to me than a rose, because that kind of beauty will fade with time
On a scale from one to ten you'll always be my dime
You're my queen
You're my hopes and my dreams
You're my angel and my dove
You're my true symbol of love

Trust me, this poem looks a lot better in color but the ink was too expensive

If you were to receive forty acres and a mule, would you trade the land in for a Lexus?

Would you feed the mule to your pit bull and use the extra cash to open up a barbershop, go shopping on 125th street and be broke by the weekend and then bitch about the economical transition that's taking place in Harlem?

Its 5:55

And on the average night, I get about four hours of sleep,
Most nights I'm trying to convey my thoughts,
Hopefully it will help upgrade this income bracket that has me limping
You thought that I was ditty bopping but I'm-Broke!
And I am not from the ghetto according to the definition
It's the slums...
And this alone gives me the ambition to fight my sleep
so one day I can fly away from this low standard of living which is on the bottom shelf
And everybody in the hood calls it "Organized Racism"
But this establishment has been in effect long before my existence and my mother already knew this
And my father already knew this
So now I'm asking, "Wassup?"

I've decided that I'm not going to sit around and bitch out forty acres and a mule
Or wait on the porch and wait for reparations
It has become idle conversation

And discussing It only slows the progress of my produc-
tivity
And if it's free... I don't want it!

I want you to understand that I'm not that grown ass man
still living in my grandmother's house
Having sex on the couch
Giving birth to bastards that run their mouth on the phone
and all they can talk about is what kind of shoes Oprah has on

Neither am I that guy breaking my neck to pay attention to
every girl with a fat butt and she arrogantly struts like the world
rotates around her Vee
But I can't see me paying some chick's car note
Or house note while she sits home watching the soaps all
day and gossiping with her girlfriend about how she's going to
spend my money on my payday!

If things got that bad I'd rather beat my meat and keep my
cash in my pocket because the end result is still goin' to be the
same
A Nut!

Call me a nut but I just can't see me sitting on the bench in
this game called life and live it complacent as a second-class
citizen, always at the bottom of the barrel waiting for leftovers

Left with this decaying thought in the back of my mind, that
life is just a bitch and this is all that I deserved!
Or left waiting for the author of this life to call cut to this
complex script-ure, rewrite it and give life a brighter outcome
That's just why I don't believe in nothing that my five
senses can't conceive or my five fingers can't touch, like luck or

Lotto or a mystery god
Because this is just a man made world and it's materialistic
And it's always going to show favoritism to the wealthy and everybody right handed

I live among the working poor and it was never intended for me to live high on the hog
And the closest that I'll ever get to enjoying something substantial is if I can create an artificial substance and then get the world dependent upon it... then charge an arm and leg for it

Or just take the easy way out
and that's to go to the closest liquor store, get drunk and put my mind in la la land, while the powers that be, the ones that run this cold ass city just sit on their asses and laugh about how they keep me in limbo with a bogus lease stating that their going to increase my rent
along with the phone bill, Credit cards, Con Ed, Cable and a Cab ride to nowhere!

So now you know why New Yorkers walk around with their faces in a knot and they never speak

It's because we are all in the same boat!
It's because we're up to our necks in bills, along with the begging ass bums and relatives that think that they need my money more then I do
And I feel for you Brother but I can't feed my family and every grown ass man that's got a song and dance

Especially if he has two hands and feet
just like me!!!

Get busy Bruh: and stop blaming everybody for our condition and using our lack of not having as an excuse to do the belligerent things that we do to one another

like the mugging, the stealing, pissing in the stairwell,

Spitting on the elevator buttons,

Letting your dog shit up the whole sidewalks

And allowing your bad ass children to be so disrespectful just because you think they are so cute!

You can't teach the youth that they can just sit at home, pray and wait for your ship to come in

You're going to have to jump off of the boat and swim in shark-infested waters just like the foreigners do

So get up and make it happen!!!

The Answer

Ladies Night... Remember?

Her name was Cindy
She preferred to be called Cinnamon
"Cindy, that name sounds so funny to me," she'd say. "Look at me, dark as I am with a name like that",
Cinnamon was a couple of years younger than me but her rough past added years to her thoughts and her ideas
Slow love songs
They sometimes reminded me of a wake or a funeral and I would be viewing my own body
I've died a thousand times listening to her story
The abuse she endured in the name of love
Mental abuse
Mental scars are the kind of scars that dictated her actions and gave reason to some of her ways
Too bad Love doesn't have an insurance policy
True love doesn't need it,
I can see myself falling for her
I just don't want her to use her past to judge me
I want to be the life preserver that slave ships never had
I want to free her from the past and I promised her that I'll never call her Cindy...

This is that Bama kind of love, Continue on next page...

AND NOW SHE'S GOT THIS BEAT GOING OFF INSIDE OF ME!!!

SHE'S PUT THIS ITCH INSIDE OF MY PALM AND EVERY POEM THAT I WRITE SEEMS TO BE CENTERED AROUND HOW NEAT SHE KEEPS HER EYEBROWS AND NOW I FIND MYSELF DOING THINGS THAT MACHO MEN SAID "MEN SHOULD NOT DO, Like... watching the cooking channel and writing poetry"

MAAAAAAAAAAANNNNNNN I've even thought about getting rid of my *RED NOSE PIT BULL* and getting me a fluffy-little-poodle

She's got this style that some might think is a little off beat
She dresses like she's only "21" but back in 1970
Cinnamon wears her hair in an Afro,with an Afro pick in her back pocket and she can block the aggressive nature of a charging African honeybee, with her earth tone lip gloss

One day she stood in this karate stance with her knees slightly bent
She had her left hand in front of her right and her fingers were in this cup position, and they were shut real tight!
She then moved her right foot in front of her left and while taking in a deep breath Cinnamon let out a loud "EEEEEEEEEE YYYAAAAHHH!"
Simultaneously while taking a backwards swing with her right hand, Cinnamon split the wind in to "2"

Then she looked at me with one of her eyebrows higher then the other and I felt as if she was my schoolteacher and I was her student

63

And she said to me, "BLUE, these things that you see me do, I catch you marveling over them, yet to me it's all miniscule. And you can do them too if want to"

And I said, "Stop playing!"

Then Cinnamon said, "No, it's true Blue and if you drop your seed into this fertile soil, it's possible we can make two of you."
And I said, "Who me?"

And Cinnamon said, "Yes U and if we have a boy we'll name him *Double U...*"

So each day my baby and me would meet over by this old picket fence where the grass grew high
And we would kick off our sneakers and roll up our blue jeans and just walk bare foot down this unpaved dirt road
And she would have the blanket and I would have the basket and we would always find ourselves on our backs -bending the blades of grass with the sun in our faces
And there I was, apologizing to the wind for all the times it snatched my hat
And the rain, for all the times it delayed the baseball games
And everything else that I had ever bad mouthed when life just didn't seem to go my way
And her chest was like a nest and it was the best place to rest my head and her hand was in my hand
And her T-shirt matched my T-shirt
And we smelled like mint!
And lemongrass!
And pollen!
And fresh baked bread!
And that was just a statement to the world that she is my

owns and I'm is her owns,   MAN!

And on our way home, Cinnamon and I would pick apples
and berries from the surrounding trees and bushes because my
baby had promised me that she was going to bake me some apple
pies and blueberry jam and she did!

And you better not go and tell her that I said
this!!!

BUT IT TASTED HORRIBLE! ! !

But you know what?

I liked it!

Because I know that pie and jam was touched by the same
hand that holds that hairbrush -when my baby tries to imitate her
favorite singer

And she tries to sing her favorite song

And bless her heart

And you better not go and tell her that I said this...

BUT SHE SOUNDS HORRIBLE!!!

But you know what?

I liked it!

Because I know if those notes weighed a ton, Cinnamon
would hold 'em for her hero, which is me!!!

And some men wish that they had a girl like this, but that's
a big if and they continue to talk but the point they miss

See Cinnamon is not a perfect 10 but to me she's close
And it really doesn't matter what you think
Ya wanna know why?
Because I like it!!!

Women call the shots

The Oblique Hints

I AM NOT, the man that feels that there is no value to a woman... and her only purpose is to be my incubator

But I honestly gave it some thought when she told me how much she liked my eyes

I'll even go so far as to admit that I am just a trick, addicted to her thighs

:The Oblique Hints of Women:

And the sweet aromatic scent of her body oil was always so intense that she... always left this funny taste in the roof of my mouth

At times I just wanted to let my taste buds run my life and start eating like I was going to the electric chair

I'm always taken by how easy she's able to look right through me but in particular the way she sends my blood rushing through my system

Split seconds apart- but seemingly spontaneous, we both agreed to take a rest from the nightly rough stuff

And instead of watching television, we let the television watch us

In and out of our mix and doing all kinds of flips and getting stuck, like dogs she screams out another man's name

Then she looks out the corner of her eyes checking to see if I was upset, but I wasn't... I kind of liked it!

I mean... its o.k. to let her fantasies take her away from reality as long as she knows you can't see the moon if there was no sun

Sugar, I am just the 2 because you are the one

You can carry me in your front pocket and I would jump at your beckoning
You can put the murder weapon in my possession and I'll take the fall 4 you... AS LONG AS YOU NEVER FORGET TO HOLD ME DOWN

But for now, just feed me some salmon croquette and some Karo syrup and a couple of slices of whole wheat toast, and I'm straight
I'll break my fast on the leftovers
And in the morning we can watch the flowers stand in formation and salute the sun
You can put your head against my chest and feel the drum that beats 4 U

Lady if I had one wish - I would hustle for time
and I'd take all that I could carry
I'd fill my front pockets with hours and my back pockets with days and I'd spend them only with you!
All for the oblique hints
And the sweet aromatic scent of your body oil
That's always so intense
That it just keeps leaving this funny taste in the roof of my mouth...

The Answer

The Remix

And here I am, a poet struggling to make ends meet
Surviving off of the food stuck in my teeth
spending my spare time begging for tooth picks
And she was, she was this - Sweet-Sticky-Thing!
And she has me thinking, Who's the silly man that does not
appreciate the ordinary way his lady smells when she gets out of the
shower
The odd shapes of her perfume bottles and the way she neat-
ly folds her pajamas in the morning
She can burn the Jell-O, but I'm cool with that
She takes three minutes to cook minute rice, *but so what?*
All you have to do is add a little sugar
And milk
and butter
and a little cinnamon
and a sprig of mint

She could set the sky on fire and have my cloths
smelling like smoke
Smoke can be stuck in my nose

Everywhere I go smells like smoke, *but so what?*

Lady I can't lie, I just want to lay underneath you
I want to wake up smelling like you

I want your scent to be on me so strong that the dog thought that I was you
And you thought that I was the dog...
trying to eat your cat!

You can take a plug of my hair - go to the local witch doctor - work your craft and watch me kill a rock for you!

Watch me put air conditioners on these city streets and cool off these girls that try to dress as hot as you!

Let me cook for you and we can eat breakfast - tonight

We can sit at the table naked, get into a food fight then use our mouths to clean up this mess

Or better yet we can just cut through the chase
clear off the kitchen table and get-it-on
right-here!!!

Lady, I have to admit that sometimes I intentionally try to get you upset so you can tell me to *kiss-Your-Ass*...

And before you would know it, I'm on my knees, taking everything that you say literally

Stop me if I'm moving too fast

I'll be happy if you let me give you a pedicure
It's not that you need it!
I just want to paint your toenails in your favorite color while I read you poems about you and me
And I'll entitle this one '*WE*'

That's because you and me,*We* give the example of what a relationship should be

You and me *we* give the inspiration to write love songs

It be those the kind of fairy tales when things never go wrong,

and w*e* know they sometimes do between me and you but *we* would never air out our dirty laundry in the public and make ourselves the subject of mockery

We can watch the moon slide across the sea while *we* take shelter under each other shadows and a blanket of kisses that will send chills up our spine

We can wear our hickeys like tattoo's

And a tattoo will be taboo if we didn't give them to one another

I can splash on that new cologne that smell like a new Cadillac with only 16 miles on the dash and you can wear that perfume that smells like money but taste like mint

So what's up?

a dead fly

Love Is?

They kiss me in my ear...
And they play in my hair
They show me so much attention that I have to fight them
off
Flies...
Flies show me love because love has become the bullshit
that I accidentally stepped into while I was walking through the
park
I now wear a pair of shades just to hide the faces of the pret-
ty women that I encounter and I try to judge their character by the
way they shake my hand
My girl, well, she's gone now
She stormed out in a rush and she took my ego with her
She engraved her name at the threshold of my bedroom,
killing all possibilities of me finding someone new
Now my perception of doubt is like this little woman
that lives in the dark corners of my mind...*AND SHE JUST SHITS ALL
OVER MY MOTIVATION!*

But I have an apartment full of flies
And I'm going to train them to be my soldiers
They will be my spies *and I'm going to send them out to
invade the privacy of her home!*

She claimed that I was a dog

But then that would make her the dogcatcher, and since I'm
no bitch, it's only natural that I'd be attracted to the opposite sex

But sometimes I feel like faking my death
Or just holding my breath
Or just standing in the corner motionless

BUT I DON'T THINK SHE'D CARE!!!

Maybe I should just move from this state that I now live in?
Or is it just the state and condition that she left my mind in?

She stated her claim when she stamped her name on my head and she left me for dead!
Now all kinds of crazy shit continues to run through my head!
She must have put the mojo on my mind

My life use to seem so simple but now my bed is hard
I've been eating stale bread that's hard
I've been eating aborted chicken and now I can't believe that it's not butter, taste good!!!

Well if I am not in control, then that means that I am out of control
That just means that I am a slave fulfilling your purpose
Hell is a condition underneath the ozone and gravity is a reality
And in spite of all your bull... when you come down
I will still be here just to prove
that I'm just a fly
in love with your shit...

Miss Gravity

There's a slow leak in the center of my earth and days seem to rotate so stagnant

I sit oblique from a baseless relationship with no substance trying to remember how things use to be

I remember when we sat around the campfire conversing about the stars and the universe and she brought up the subject

"Who would get eaten first if we ran out of food in the wilderness"?

She doesn't know it...

but I bite my nails a lot and that makes me feel like a cannibal...

When a man takes a woman out on a first date, It's really like an open contract

That's when he lays his cards on the table and it's a test on his character...is he going to pick up the tab?

Or at least make an attempt,   and I did!

I couldn't wait to meet your mama's man!

I couldn't wait to shake his hand!

I couldn't wait to walk in his shoes

And produce another you!

And we were supposed to go walking bare foot on the beaches of the Eastern seaboard with the hopes of doing the same thing on the West coast...

Life is a hurt sport and pain is The Great Persuader

And once a man puts his hands on a woman, then he's

only proving that he's losing

So all of my ideas of a good relationship / I keep to myself
And they sit in the pit of my stomach
Next to my will and my pride
And I chase it with a shot of liquor
While it gets filtered through my liver
And it feels like I'm living in hell

As I wait to die and go to hell,
Because once you're dead you don't know that you're
dead, So what the Hell???

Every 28 days, my girl gets this not so fresh feeling, and
she has to be putting it in my food, in the tomato sauce
Because she has my backbone weaker than a string of
spaghetti
And every time I get ready to stand up
I BLOW IT!

I PROMISE MYSELF THAT I'M GOING TO DO THIS
BUT I END UP DOING THAT!
And she knows it!

Then other men and my so-called friends start to make a
mockery of my state of mind and money doesn't rhyme with cash
But I put some in the stash if she had the time
And it's ok for her to jack off
There's just nobody to hug her once she crosses the finish
line
That girl and I, we put the star on 69
I nicknamed her 99 for all her attributes
I'm torn between wanting you
But not necessarily needing you

Here I am, a man that thinks so much about being in control and I'm ready to lose all my cool points just to get lost in your space

But I'll give you room for space and space for air
And air for room whenever you sneeze or snore
Or even shut the bathroom door to take a shit!!!

I've never been a woman before
So how would I know what makes her happy, if she doesn't tell me
If it was left up to the subjects that men discuss in our circle, I heard the best place to kiss a woman is on the Brooklyn Bridge

The creator has to have a sense of humor
For what reason would he go and create a woman so fine?

I guess so he can just sit back and laugh at this foolish look on my face every time I see your face
I just want to be that book that wraps you up in the wings of a love story and it leaves you compelled to lick your thumb as you flip the page

I want to be that man that you thought you met by accident
But in actuality it was the law of cause and effect
I woke up late and missed the bus and I caught the train and bumped into you
I was born for you!
Then sometimes I wonder if I'm worthy
Uncertainty pulling me by my coattail whispering in my ear, "do I deserve thee?"

Miss Gravity please don't take what I say lightly

Corner Stores

The reason that this relationship is so rich is because my thoughts on loving you are so fancy

You are my twin

I am you

And you are me and it can be proven at any point and time

So I'm begging you, Miss Gravity ...please let me down lightly

Haiku
Unlady Like

The girl that I like
is very unlady like

Yet, perfect for me

Twisted

*A Poem inspired by the Attractive Lady
on the number 2 Train*

Her locks had me twisted…
and once I stopped spinning

I found myself, trying to find myself…

Don't spend more than one dollar to bury me!

don't know where I'll spend my last breath, but if you don't do anything else tonight... just remember this voice

Just remember that this body is nothing but a suit

It's something that I slipped into so I could mingle amongst the general public for a short length of time and once it expires, this skin will return to the essence

So if you were wise...

You wouldn't spend more than one dollar to bury me

You would be better off going to the nearest corner store, get a cardboard box and flip me in it

And if that's too much to ask of you, then leave me where you found me and I'll soak into the earth like road kill

Just don't get pimped by the funeral parlor when they try to convince you that you got to spend your hard earned money to send me off to a better place and there's no proof that I'm going to get there

Heaven and Hell is a condition!

Something that you experience while you are living

The after life is a myth that was spoon fed to the masses of black people, so that we would always have that, *"Turn the other cheek mentality"*

Now here we are walking in the hood like passive vegetarians, being consumed by carnivores in this land of the lost

Call me the F-O-U-L bird when I say, "make money players, learn to play this American game- feed your face and your family and keep your collection plate money in your pocket or spend it on the living

Because the dead can't do a damn thing with it!"

The Urban Look

:Part 1:

:It's that pissy stench that gets stuck in your nose and that is to let you know when you're getting closer to the zoo
But the minute you get to see the animals eating and drinking in their natural habitat, you get overwhelmed with so much excitement you don't notice the stench anymore...

(And I bet that's the thought that goes through the tourists mind when they come cruising through the hood, looking at us like we're crabs in a barrel)

nd every time I pick up this pen it's like releasing myself, Pretend that this note pad is like the rest room Step back because I'm about to drop some deep shit

If Poppa was a rolling stone then what would happen if he ran into Miss Jones, chances are that they would produce me
The trick baby
And it's the fairy tale books that lead to foreplay and it always ends up screwing the people!

And that's what has them all brain washed, while they blindly follow the pied piper to the next corner, like it's the second coming of the Lord
Yet, it's called the style
But I knew that they weren't going too far out of the hood with those flip flops on your feet

81

And your white socks, shorts, the icy white T-shirt and the du-rag

I thought that you were going to the barbershop

There's one on every corner in this neighborhood but the brothers with the cornrows got business moving kind of slow

And just when Jordan would bring that bald headed trend in back in style...the twin towers were destroyed...

Therefore his come back press conference wasn't important

This is the neck of the woods where Little Red Riding Hood raised her babies to dress like Bloods

They rock red bandannas yet they bitch about racial profiling

The "five O" wear blue like the Crips so if you're on the run you better cover your face, there might be cameras in this place, ya never know

Throw your government name in the garbage and get an alias from the alphabet

But JZ and AZ are already taken

Call yourself God or Dog and use it in reverse... Plus it's universal

Freedom has a price and your pockets have to be deep

That's why it's the working poor that always end up in jail

You must make money players

Learn to play this American game

Feed your face and your family and send all your children to school and teach them how to steal... *Legally*

Because that's the American way!

The Urban Look :Part 2:

Bulletproof Corner Stores

Street protocol sometimes has me on the wrong side of the law, and this has to be city of god...

I come from nothing with nowhere to go
Nothing grows here but preconceived notions and misconceptions so what can the government take from me... when I ain't got shit...

I got a closet full of clothes, bad credit and my speech impediment is always taken out of context
But check it...even when I'm walking backwards it's still considered a step in the right direction

I'm like a rapper residing in a roach infested tenement building
It's no bigger then an auction block and the only way out, is to sell my soul and appease these critics that don't know a damn thing about me... so what do I do?
I stay...because this ain't my life

This is just some shit that I'm going through right now
It's just my bad hair day

It's like those holistic black men that twist and lock their hair as if that's a prerequisite to date white girls from the Village

And this ghetto life ain't nothing but a vicious cycle like the steam piss that comes from sewer 7, Pipe 11
while everyone in the urban area has this belief that the best things in life are free but they don't walk like that
And poor people... they don't shop like that

Now ask me who fucks us the best in a fuckin' contest and I'll tell you that I got living this paycheck to paycheck lifestyle down to a science by paying the rent first, the phone bill last and everybody on my block has Jiggie cable

This is where bulletproof Corner Stores never stop to take a breath...and you can catch a contact from the gun smoke...
You just stepped into a tight chest situation where elbow-room is overrated and the scent of roach spray just might get you homesick...

It was 212 West 129th Street
That's where the needle skipped on the family that broke the record for all of those times the mice left holes in the loaf of bread, while the roaches were playing dead like raisins... and they were backstroking in my bowl of oatmeal

I had a good stomach back then...
It was during those days of free sex, good loving had a price and cold chilling was an understatement

We use to get dressed up... just to go to bed...wrapped under blankets and coats and then jumped up sweating from the cries of an Alley cat in heat
Then by the time you've reached the age of 2 or 3 you

become numb to this noise and if you move down south the silence leads to your insomnia

This all took place when Harlem was an armpit...

It was right before gentrification began to give this modern day Jericho a face-lift

It's when the middle class never came past 59th Street on the Uptown D- train... and a seat was guaranteed

We sat around a lit cigarette that served as light and heat and we were like survivors of lead paint poison…
and second hand smoke

It felt like we were serving time... for killing time

Fuck sheep!
We were counting Pit Bulls to get some sleep
You might see a blind man try to talk his way out of a fist-fight after being accused of looking at somebody the wrong way

But I was considered the repulsive one… Crying ugly

I'm upset because I gotta' dry my socks in front of the stove with my underwear on the radiator
and I started saving all of my asthma pumps, because somebody was telling me that they're gonna be worth a lot of money some day!

People call me crazy but padded walls in these housing projects couldn't stop the source of what I write from or to
It's like music!
It's the equivalent to getting on the subway train early in the morning and listen to straphangers make an attempt to adjust to this claustrophobic situation the best way that they know how...

And that's by sitting on the train with their hands over their heads as they hide their faces and suck their teeth... all at the same time... at the sight of my face

But strange as that may sound, it's music to my ears

It was also a song written in a New York minute, copy written the old fashion way by the same group of people that coined the catch phrase "Watch my feet, Don't ask me for shit and Get the Hell out of here!"

Which can be taken as a question or a demand depending on the tone of the voice!

So whenever you flat foot your way around my way, you'll see more barbershops then bookstores and there's a pet shop right across the street from the housing projects...

Now this shit is crazy, because you would think, that after living in this claustrophobic situation for so long... someone would show some compassion for the Goldfish in a bowl with no where to go… but in circles

Or the caged up Black bird with a broken soul!!!

This is not the concrete Jungle... It's a Bulletproof Circus
It's where grown men walk around with cartoons on their sweat suits and Gucci Nike's shooting free throws for free cheese
And I keep saying to myself, "I gotta' get out of this place!"

The Urban Look :Part 3:

Urban Renewal

You can ride the number 10 bus from point A to point B and watch the buildings begin to drift... Uptown!

This is the minority section of the city

And 8th Avenue is like a river that pumps the blood into this borough, but if you thought that apples couldn't bleed... Ya betta' ask somebody

Or better yet you can save time and just ask me, and we can play Tit for Tat as I kindly ask you to remove your socks and shoes from your feet and let your soles touch these sidewalks as you muster up the strength to relate to this hard knock life

But you should already know the official particulars

It was the quick money and dirty hands

Crack came into the neighborhood and sucked the life out of the city, killed two birds with one stone and sometimes it seems like nothing can save us!

Some say I should pray... but a prayer sometimes seems like it's nothing but a nick-name for an overrated jump shot that was slowly released from the fingertips of that high school kid down the block named Moses

And I don't know if you notice it or not, but my neighborhood has more churches then schools

In fact there's a Church on all four corners surrounding the housing projects like a fort and it's got the residents trapped

And every school playground has a child named Moses that wants to jump and handle his way out the hood

Yet they allow pressure from the atmosphere and their peers to hamper their ability to improve their skills

And like Moses they'll be just another story of a child that came close... But never made it!

So welcome to life is a bitch!

And this is the urban look

This is where in the summer time we attend picnics on dead blades of grass and broken glass on the playground glitters like fragments of stardust... under the night lights

This is what the tourist break their necks to come see...

They really want to learn how we continue to exist on the inside of the sun

This is where there's an erotic section in the New York leasing laws that allows the landlord to screw the tenants anytime he wants and there's nothing you can do about it

And urban renewal wants everybody out!

This is where emergency rooms are ran like something from the medieval times and medical students are taught the craft of milking Medicare cards immediately

This is where Mecca sits next door to the methadone clinic and a malpractice lawsuit allows a bum, *The Once In A Lifetime* chance to dress nice if he doesn't mind having the wrong finger amputated...

But the funny thing about this is... somebody will see that dude with the missing finger... and they'll think that it looks cool... And before you know it... that shit is gonna' be a new style
And I can see the scenario now:

Some cool dude will be hanging out on the street corner boasting to his friends about his incident and he'll hold up his hand and say something like, "Yo, check it out son, I just got my finger cut off... This shit look hot... right?"

Then his partner is gonna' answer back and say something like,"Yeah, Yeah I'm feeling that son... Watch tomorrow I'm gonna' get all of my fingers cut off! But first I'm gonna' get my right thumb cut off and then I'll get my left index finger cut off and when the ho's see this... they gone be sweating me!
Watch son!"

And you might be thinking to yourself that this poem is deep...   But it's not!

Deep is the way a Lady will stand up to her Man...
Yet she'll run from a mouse...

But then again, that's not Deep...
Deep is the way girls only seem to show interest in me when they see me with another girl...
So I started hanging out with lesbians...
And we pick up girls together...

But then again... that's not Deep...
Deep is the way this young dude asked me, "What's the quickest way to get from here to Rikers Island?"

And I told him, "You gotta' take the D Train to 34th street and throw a brick through Macy's window!"

Now that's Deep!

So whenever the movie script calls for that urban look, the camera crew comes to my block
And graffiti is always in the background of some cat's portfolio
Sometimes with the letters spray painted in calligraphy
Just like the fonts on the cover of the Bible
and survival is the code we live by

But let me tell you something about Black people

We make this struggling shit look easy!

We do it so well we even named a dance after it...and it was called...The Hustle!
But check this out: I heard how ole girl from down the block had deliberately checked her child in to a dysfunctional class just so she can receive a disability paycheck
And she neglects to check the progress of the child
because she has to check into the local strip club and she hustles
She works her ass off...*LITERALLY*

She struggles to make ends meet... Up until the weekend where nothing is free in this country except... flyers...and garbage...

Umpteen years later, here I is...The dysfunctional black bastard

Born in this rat race city that just so happens to consist of human participants

And I got a can't wait mentality!

I got three friends with asthma... one with sickle cell and a chipped tooth...

We call him Big Mike

Mike only stands 5'5" but he likes to carry a pistol when he's pissed off

So what choice do I have?

I call him Big Mike...just like everybody else...and everybody in here knows someone just like me!

Jaywalking is just imbedded into my genetic make up and sometimes when I'm crossing the street I just feel like saying, "Fuck this red light...

I wish a yellow cab would hit me!"

I want it to hit me so bad...but not hard...because sometimes it seems like a Lawsuit is the only way out of this deep dark ditch that we call debt... and want... and need... and greed

And all of this drama takes place in that section of the city where English is the second language, spanish is the first and I rehearse it when the Latina mama's walk this way

But most times folks in general act like it hurts to speak and hospitality is played out like a black and white TV

This is that section of the city where you never see the big dogs that run this place up until it's time to win the Black vote

That's when they'll go visit the local Black church while smiling in our faces, they'll be cracking jokes behind our backs... Talking about how we got the Holy Ghost, and we wuz sweating

out these perms from under our Sunday hat!!!

And that's cool... but all I wanna know is... where was the Holy Ghost when Kunta Kinte was getting his toes chopped off?

Where was the Holy Ghost when the cable company sent the final cut off notice and the scented candles were used to dilute the stench of last nights sex fiesta that we called the rent party!

My name is BLUE and this is that grits and gravy kind of poetry!

This poetry is like that old can of chicken grease that's been sitting on top of the stove and only the Lord knows how long it's actually been there...But it always made the best fried chicken It always made the best pork chops and the best biscuits...
.

And this is the kind of poem that taught me how to stretch my eggs with milk... stretch my milk with water... and my water with sugar..

This is that getting your ass whipped with a extension cord kind of poem...
This is the poem that said computers are going to run this planet and people are living too long...
Anthrax is nothing but AIDS condensed into a powder because cocaine wasn't killing yuppies quick enough...

Crack cocaine was invented with the intent for people to get addicted then be delinquent on their rent...then they could be kicked out on the street and make room for the aristocrat
If you don't believe me, just decipher the subliminal billboard messages when you get on the subway train in the morning

This is that, "I'm tired of living like a sardine," kind of poem...

This is that big ass baby carriage that blocks the subway doors in the morning kind of poem...

This is that one mama, three babies, and three different baby daddy's kind of poem...

This is that poem that wants to tell that guy that has been dating that girl for three weeks that she's not having sex with him because she's still having sex with her ex-boyfriend...

This is that poem that said the only reason those tour buses come through the hood taking pictures is so they can go back home and spread the propaganda that the brothers from another planet are easy to pimp...

That's why this neighborhood is flooded with bootleg batteries, Yo-Yo's for a dollar, out dated chicken, and soul food joints owned by illegal aliens that think that I'm a lazy American...

This is that poem that wants a religion that's going to put some cash in my pocket and not a pamphlet telling me what Hell is like...

This is that lopsided living room kind of poem...

This is that Black and White TV with aluminum foil wrapped around the hanger that we use as an antenna kind of poem...

This is that instant oatmeal... oatmeal in an instant, Quick grits... Minute Rice... Cool Aid and no sugar

Low fat butter

Low fat fat

Spoiled baby

Nagging husband

Gossiping grandma

Back firing gun

Short fuse firecracker that blew up in your hand...

The crack head mechanic that messed up your car worse then it already was...

And the women that act like crack heads, when they insist on braiding my hair every time I get off the D - train on 125th Street

This is that poem that said there has got to be a hidden clause in the Holy Quran that states, 'Muslims are not allowed to eat or touch pork, Unless they run a bodega' like the ones in Harlem, and Watts, and Crenshaw, and East St. Louis, and the Alabama Projects in Paterson, New Jersey

Or the Paterson Projects in the Bronx, New York

That's where lotto and liquor stores go hand and hand and everybody feels as though the brothers in the hood have to pay for every world war that has taken place on their soil

So the store clerks be in the stores cheating the children out of their change

(*but the children do go in the stores and shoplift, And the bad part about it is the parents know that their children are in the store shoplifting, and they won't say shit*)

But then the store wants to charge me fifty cents for a 37 cents United States postal stamp.

The Hood is where the neighborhood restaurant can make an order of some chopped up bullshit that will melt in your mouth and cat soup is on the lunch special menu but you gotta' ask for it under the name "Woo-hop"

And while I wait for my order I can be entertained by some jiggie 4 year old little boy with a pair of pants that can fit me

And he's doing the shake and reciting the lyrics to every rap song that comes on the radio but when I asked him to recite his alphabet, the boy can't get pass the letter E

And I'm thinking to myself, *I bet if he practiced the alphabet with a Puff Daddy remix, then he'll get the shit right*

And this is that kind of poem and...

The Urban Look :Part 4:

Project Zero

come from that Crop, that the government paid farmers not to grow

It's like the projects that doctors have been running on birth control and when Daddy got fed up and ran out the back door
I grew up Out-Of-Control, in the New York City housing Projects…

You call me that zero, but I was produced by generation X
I'm standing in a circle surrounded by men that fit my description and we got caught up in a conversation and they asked me would I care to elaborate on what I think about the state of this world?
And my reply was...
Scientist are trying to dictate the weather when they tamper with the sun
They've been sending satellites into orbit so they can spy on me and son
And it's got brothers in the hood kind of bugged out
It's got grown men acting like boys and call each other son
And home boy
and bad boy
and hot boy and ghetto boy...

Boys make babies - then run
Women keep saying that all men are dogs

In The Middle Of The Block

But they are the one's that raised them
single handedly in the New York City housing projects

And I can just tell by the looks on your face
that the first time that you saw my face you probably
thought that I was some kind of athlete
or an entertainer
And I'd be standing up here bragging about my forthcoming
CD
And now everybody wants me to come to their church
Meet their pastor
Kiss their baby
Sit in the front rostrum of the pulpit and get moved by the
spirit
And then give all the glory to God for my success
And in this great line of divine, of course my beloved mother would be mentioned next but when someone asks me about my father I'm supposed to say, "Fuck him!
Because this is what everyone expects of me!

And in my *Kinder - Garden* state of mind, I was supposed to be that sponge absorbing all the negative bullshit that society has to say about the man that gave me life, just because he's not able to stand next to some world famous crack head that the big screen uses as their standard of a macho hunk
So when the going was good... I was good

And when things got bad, I was bad just like my dad

I also have this funny shaped head like my father
I'm flat footed like my father
I'm clumsy like my father
I talk too much like my father
And I'm Always saying the wrong shit at the wrong time...

JUST LIKE MY FATHER!

But someone must have been hoping that I would be that cute little baby boy with the good folks hair and the good folks eyes

And I was supposed to be that glue that seals my parents bond and keep this love thing together for at least 18 years

But once reality sets in and I'm another mouth to feed and I'm also going to need new shoes

Or a new t-shirt, and a new toothbrush, that's when this loving relationship suddenly turns to hate and it can't make it pass the first year and before you know it here comes another baby and another baby and another baby

And now we are like the ghetto version of the Bradys with a bunch of babies and baby daddy's

And we all have different grains of hair, different shades of skin, and our complexion is perfect for a system that uses us for target practice and labels us the underclass

The overweight

The obese

The big- boned

They call me that light brown African offspring and some seem to think that all we like to eat is cheap Chinese food which is nothing but chicken wings and fried rice with salt and pepper

Extra ketchup

Fish on Fridays

Government cheese

Peanut butter

Powdered milk

Churches Fried Chicken

Kansas Fried Chicken

Kentucky Fried Chicken

Kennedy Fried Chicken

Mama and Papa's Fried Chicken

His and Hers Fried Chicken

King Fried Chicken
Queen Fried Chicken
Crown Fried Chicken
Royal Fried Chicken
Crispy Fried Chicken
Extra crispy Fried Chicken
Sister Shirley's from the fifth floor fried chicken and expired boxes of some sweet ass cereal with no nutritional value that you can buy in the slums at the 99 cent store which comes out to a $1.07 after taxes

And the test is to see how I'm going to react when a customer goes in to the corner store and tells Muhammad "Salaam Alikum, make me a ham and cheese sandwich with oil and vinegar, salt and pepper, lettuce, hold the tomatoes, mayo on both sides of the bread, AND YO! GIVE ME MY FREE SODA!"

Then he puts your sandwich in a brown paper bag and soon as you get out of the stores front door you throw the bag in the street and you look at me like I should pick it up

Then when you walk out of your front door the next day you wonder why the neighborhood looks so fucked up

But then you want to blame the government for not allocating more funds to send someone to come and pick that shit up...
And the project is to see how well I survive off of a fixed income
I've been wearing name brand clothes, made by unknown designers, so that makes me a model for no one...
I do not have time to attend fashions shows on the runway of a subway platform

And this has got to be the city where everyone is asleep

except for the dead and me
And we stayed up half the night dancing to a beat that was originated by the elderly and it was called Be- bop
Then Doo Wop
and now it's Hip Hop

But like I have already told you, I come from that crop like the one that farmers were paid not to grow
It's like that project that doctors have been running on birth control and when Daddy got fed up and left out of the back door
I grew up Out-Of-Control in the New York City housing projects

Some call me a zero
 but I was produced by generation X,
I'm standing in the center of a circle surrounded by men that fit my description and we got caught up in a conversation and they asked me if I cared to elaborate on what I think is wrong with the state of the world
And my reply was:

I'm here to let you know that I am the bad apple
The fruit that you all produce
and if you don't like it just keep in mind that I did not fall too far from the tree...

Haiku
Good Hair?

What's more important?

The texture of your child's hair

Or what's in their head?

Telephone Love

*A Poem inspired by the Attractive Lady
on The Bronx Bound 4- Train*

Hold me...
The way that u hold your cell phone...

Up to your ear
and close to your mouth...

Telephone Lust

*A Poem inspired by the Attractive Lady
on The Manhattan bound D - Train*

Put your cell phone on vibrate
Sit it on your lap...

And I'll call you when I'm coming...

Elbowroom Is Overrated

Monday mornings are the canvas
Mud is the theme and we make love in earth tones
while giving birth to raindrops

I'm loving you to death, lady…
In a watercolor kind of way

Brooklyn Girl

*A Poem inspired by the Attractive Lady
on The Brooklyn bound Q-train*

She sat across from me with a vintage leather jacket on
She had her hair in cornrolls and her jeans were rolled up
like a cowgirl...

Home girl had eyes like a six shooter and I wanna tell her
how fine she looks

but I'm afraid she'll shoot me

Conversation Peace

By my home girl, Andrea Newman

Say Brotha…

I was just thinking that maybe u and I could get a rap
U know sit down and talk about this and that
Discuss our lives and what it means to be Black…
Just u and me!

I mean…
I've often wondered from a distance
What it would be like if we became victims…of the same
space and opportunity?
How much would we have in common?
What's your bag? And I'll tell u mine…
U know…it'll just be 2 people sharing a common chemistry with
the bottom denominator as being…
Conversation with no hidden agenda, brotha…just a rap
See…
I like long walks in the park, my zodiac sign is Taurus and
I enjoy horse back riding..
And I'm smiling cause I'm just jiving…

And for fear of sounding like the Jet Beauty of the Week
With those fake ass points of interests…brotha I'll be true

See, I like to write poetry, and I love to cook

And I'd like to think that I can make u smile and…
I'm a little bit rock n roll and a whole lotta soul
So brotha…..what about u?

Tell me, what do u like to do?
What holds your attention?
What are your ambitions?
And what keeps you wishing that rainy days never come
and when u rise
U always see the sun?
Yeah…I've seen u out from time to time in the public
And I've had the chance to fall into a hypnotic groove of
your voice during conversations with others and u know what?
I loved it!
How u spoke with such passion and the questions they
were asking
And how when someone passed u by….
U always took the time to say, "hi…. how u doing?"
I wanna know what's your favorite song?
And do u say the infamous…."OOOOOhhhh damn, that's
my shyt"…When it comes on…. loud over the speakers
Do u seek the truth when u listen?
And do u believe there's a higher power that rules this land
of the living?

What pisses u off brotha? …
And betta' yet…. what gets u off. Huh?
I just wanna know and allow me to make mental notes
So if any of this conversation should progress into something
more…then I'll be prepared.

What's your favorite color, red or black?
And do u ever wonder if Marcus Garvey had the right idea
about us

"Going back to the Motherland,"
And are u the type of cat to take a stand or just play the passive role?

Do u voice your opinions or allow others to take control?
Would u sell your soul for the love of money?
And are u the type that's consistent with speaking if you saw me coming....In your direction?
What's your ideal place to vacation?
Is it a long week at Disney or the island of Jamaica?
Does the type of car one drives really make a difference?
Do u live alone...with a roommate or stay with ya relatives?

Say brotha...
What's your favorite brand of sneakers?
Is it Reebok, Nike, or is it Adidas?
Now I know...I've just asked mad questions
So ya nerves I'm hoping I'm not plucking

But we grown folks have this tendency to stop communicating once we start phucking.... would you agree?

Revolutionary Rhetoric

Once the D.J. finish searching the milk crate for the best gospel song and I'm finish this poem, this place might get quiet as the local mortuary or cemetery and easily this poem will be described as an obituary for all these dead poets that tried to knock the way that I make ends meet
And these motherfuckers don't feed me

They don't put food on my plate but every week they're the same ones that get on this stage and masturbate for the sake of a grand prize

But don't they know, that I've been doing this before there was a time limit or a two-drink minimum
And three hundred bucks is not enough to finance their war or help purchase a new fighter jet... So cut the bullshit
You kamikazes kill me with this revolutionary rhetoric

Don't you know life is a bitch, this world is flat and *what goes around comes around* is just a catch phrase
That's was just a slogan, which was forced fed to black folks, to give us hope

It's like saying, "I'll be back, or you'll see me again," or "Don't call us, we'll call you."

Basically it's really getting a warm hug after getting fucked for so many years and your tears can't persuade these racist rednecks to change their views on you

And if karma were true, the klu-klux-klan would be pickin' cotton right now

But, let's get back to you!

There should be somebody checkin' bags at the door, just to make sure you can't come in here with that cough medicine philosophy

It's that bullshit that you call poetry that puts the audience to sleep

and the individuals that can stay awake, end up leaving because they think the following poets are gonna' be wack

Like you

You should hold an open mic at your house, and invite yourself

Because no one likes what you write but yourself

And I personally feel if you have a skill that's sitting on a shelf collecting dust and you choose not to make it work for you, then fuck you!

And fuck anyone that so happens to like what you write

You wrote some bullshit poetry and the best thing you could have did was put it on CD, or DVD

You're the type of guy that would try to bootleg a bootleg C. D.

You remind me of Fredo

You remind me of some ghetto bastard sitting on the train reading "True to the Game", or at home trying to pimp the welfare system and use your body as a lotto ticket

And this is not a poetry slam, you changed it to group therapy

It's for disgruntled MCs

pretending to be poets,

hoping to say some smooth shit just to get some ass at the end of the night..